Cesky Terrier

A Guide for Owners, Prospective Owners &
Conformation Judges

ISBN-13: 9781973742630

DEDICATION

Mr. Frantisek Horak
(1909 – 1996)

Because one of one man's courage and vision …

Thank you for giving us the Cesky Terrier.

CONTENTS

ACKNOWLEDGMENTS

Cover Photo: by Loren Marino of
GCHS CH BVWBE'16 EUVW'16 CGCA
Milenka's Hector in Act Four CGCU TKA
"Hector"

1 A BRIEF HISTORY

The Cesky Terrier, also known as the Bohemian Terrier or Czech Terrier, was the vision and project of Mr. Frantisek Horak a genetic scientist in Czechoslovakia (now known as the Czech Republic). Mr. Horak worked for many years at the Academy of Science in Prague. We credit the very detailed notes of the formation of this breed to the scientific background of its creator.

Mr. Horak was a breeder of the Scottish terrier, which he used to hunt deer near his home. Mr. Horak was concerned however, about the aggressive nature of the Scotty breed when hunting in pairs. In 1934, he met some breeders of Sealyham terriers with which he had a conversation about the two breeds. It was at this time he conceived the theory that the product of crossing the two breeds (Sealyham and Scottish Terrier) could create the ideal hunting dog which would work in a pack, be agile, and could go to ground and fit in burrows too small for the Sealyham terrier.
It was not until after the Second World War in 1949, that Mr. Horak was able to do the first breeding between a Scottish Terrier bitch, Donka Lovu Zdar and a Sealyham Terrier dog, Buganier Urquelle. Unfortunately, the first offspring of this Scottish and Sealyham mating was shot by a careless hunter in 1950.

Mr. Horak however did not give up, he produced another mating between a brindle Scottish Terrier, named Scotch Rose and the Sealyham Buganier Urquelle, producing a litter of six puppies, from which the male Balda Lovu zDar was chosen.

Balda, who was brindle, was then bred back to his Scottish terrier mother Scotch Rose. From their mating Diana Lovu zDar was born, she was born black and later turned to a deep gray color and had the desired drop ears, that would become hallmarks of the breed.

Later we will get more in depth into the foundations of the breed. What is important to note is that the Cesky Terrier is an inbred breed. There are just two Lines, the 1A which is the foundation of the breed. This line has the genetic material from just three dogs. The 1B line which came about in 1972, and after the FCI gave permission to introduce one additional Sealyham terrier to the breeding of the Cesky Terrier, consists of the genetic material of the 3 foundation dogs plus this one additional Sealyham terrier and one additional dog from an impure breeding. So the entire gene pool with which to work, consists of just 3 or 5 dogs, (depending on line), and the spontaneous genetic mutations that have occurred with breeding. Therefore today the most respected breeders understand that very selective breeding to maintain the consistency, as well as the attributes of the breed standard, is a matter of 1. selection for expression of genes and 2. tracking genetic mutations.

In Mr. Horak's vision of the ideal Cesky terrier, he desired a lean, short legged terrier, with a powerful hind quarter, a chest that was narrower than the hind quarters, a moderately sized wedge shape head, legs that were just slightly longer than the Scottish terrier and suited to powerful digging and endurance. Mr. Horak desired a terrier smaller than the Sealyham that would be suited to go to ground, but still be agile enough to cover ground in the woods. The Cesky he felt should keep a silkier coat, that would be easy to maintain, and as such the Cesky terrier is never hand stripped and it is trimmed with clippers and scissoring even for the show ring. It was important that the Cesky Terrier have a temperament that was ferocious on the hunt, but also be a dog that would be easy to control and live with in the home and in a pack. Mr. Horak's desire for the Cesky was to hunt a variety of game including fox, deer, duck and wild boar, among other game.

In 1963, the Cesky Terrier was officially recognized by the Federation Cynologique Internationale (FCI, in English: World Canine Organization) Increasingly the breed spread across Europe and other parts of the world.

The Cesky Terrier was officially recognized to compete in the Terrier group in the USA by the American Kennel Club on June 30th, 2011, with the First Champion points awarded on July 1, 2011 in Maryland.

2 THINGS TO CONSIDER

The breed was created as a dog that would serve as a Working Hunter and Companion. The modern day Cesky terrier is not so different, though some excel and focus more on the companion area than others.

- As a Hunter, even today, in the Czech Republic this hardy, loyal companion, is a mighty hunter. Working along side the hunter in a multitude of ways, from tracking, to flushing, killing or being a gun dog, the Cesky is versatile, agile, and enthusiastic. They are not afraid of big game, from deer to wild boar, and are efficient in their pursuit of small game, from ducks to fowl, to rodents and badgers.

- Competitor : with an array of hunting skills it is no surprise that in modern day they excel in array of companion events. From Agility, to obedience, Rally obedience, barn hunting, earthdog, tracking, fly ball and yes these happy and quite silly terriers love to do tricks.

<u>**Traits of the Cesky Terrier:**</u>
* In the field, the rugged and persistent Cesky Terrier has more working instincts than most other terriers.

* In the home, the Cesky has a sweeter, more laid-back disposition. Indeed, the Cesky may be the mildest and easiest to handle/train of all the terriers.

* Given moderate exercise and lots of personal attention the Cesky adapts to virtually any household -- city/apartment, suburb, or farm.

* Though playful and inquisitive outdoors -- the large Cesky nose is usually glued to the ground -- the Cesky is calm indoors.

* With strangers, Cesky Terriers are usually reserved but polite, though early and consistent socialization is a must to develop and maintain this attitude.

* The Cesky is more sociable and less aggressive than most terriers. The Cesky is more powerful than similar sized terriers and young dogs often are not aware of their strength. This is where a solid foundation in training is helpful.

* Though the Cesky can be very determined and focused, the Cesky responds well to positive driven obedience training (praise or food and reinforcement by repetition and consistency).

* Just go easy on the food so that the Cesky doesn't pack on weight. This may be easier said than done, as the Cesky tends to be a food thief whose long reach, when standing on his hind legs, or 4 foot leaping ability can result in the family meal vanishing off the kitchen countertop.

* Unfortunately, it isn't only food that Cesky Terriers like to devour -- they are noted for their powerful jaw strength and destruction of toys, so it's not uncommon for them to swallow inedible objects, which may lead to some frantic evenings in the veterinary emergency room.

If you want a dog who...
- Is short-legged, long-bodied and much more muscular and more substantial than other dogs of their size
- Has a silky, straight to wavy coat of hair not fur, that doesn't shed much
- Needs only moderate exercise
- Is energetic outdoors, mellow and quiet indoors

- Compared to most other terriers, is sweeter-natured, more laid-back, and more sociable with other pets
- Is uncommon

A Cesky Terrier may be right for you.

If you don't want to deal with...
- Providing enough attention, exercise and activities to keep them satisfied
- Timidity or fearfulness when not socialized enough
- Providing early obedience training with regular reinforcement
- High Determination (prey drive)
- Frequent brushing, combing, and clipping
- Waiting lists (hard to find)

A Cesky Terrier may NOT be right for you.

Remember you can avoid or minimize some negative traits by (1) carefully choosing the right breeder and allowing the breeder to choose the right puppy for you; (2) choosing an adult dog who has already proven that he doesn't have negative traits.

<u>**More traits and characteristics of the Cesky Terrier**</u>
If I were considering a Cesky Terrier, I would be most concerned about...

1. **Providing enough exercise and mental stimulation.** These Smart Terriers don't need miles of running exercise, but they do need regular opportunities to vent their energy and occupy their mind.
2. **Providing enough socialization.** Cesky Terriers need extensive exposure to people and to unusual sights and sounds so that their natural caution doesn't become suspiciousness or shyness, which are difficult to live with. Also, remember that the cesky was bred as a pack dog. They want to be with their pack leader (hopefully you) as much as possible. Long absences away from you can in itself lead to lack of confidence.
3. **Determination.** Though easier to training than some other terriers, Cesky Terriers must still be taught at an early age that they are not the rulers of the world and to control their strength. The hardiness that makes them

suited to killing vermin can be challenging if they have not been given early boundaries. Cesky Terriers can be determined and manipulative. You must show them, through absolute consistency, that you mean what you say and that you are the team captain.

4. **Grooming.** To keep their coat short and free of mats, Cesky Terriers require regular brushing and washing. The Cesky Terrier has hair not fur, just imagine if you went a whole month without washing your hair. While not required to wash daily it is recommended that they be washed every 10 to 14 days. Clipping and trimming regularly will also help to keep them clean and tangle free.

5. **Finding one.** Cesky Terriers are rare in the United States, with fewer than 50 new Cesky Terrier puppies born each year. Compare that to over 60,000 new Golden Retriever puppies!

Consider adopting an ADULT Cesky Terrier...
When you're acquiring a Cesky Terrier **PUPPY**, you're acquiring **potential** -- what he one day will be.

But when you acquire an **ADULT** dog, you're acquiring what he already **IS** and you can decide whether he is the right dog for you based on an already formed personality, which was hopefully raised under the hand of an experienced Cesky Breeder.

When looking at the health of the Cesky Terrier as a breed, it is fair to say that the starting point is and should be with the parent breeds . The Sottish & Sealyham Terriers of the 1940s, as well as the Sealyham of the 1980s. One must also take into account the naturally occurring mutations in the breed itself.

Some of the Health concerns found in the Cesky Terrier
  I.   Hip Dysplasia
       According to OFA.org statistics as of December 2018, 35% of the Xrayed Cesky Terriers have some form of Hip Dysplasia.
  II. Scotty Cramp
       A serotonin disorder which manifests as a puppy or young dog. This condition is lifelong, but can be

managed.

III. Cerebella Abiotrophy
A late onset disorder, Cerebella Abiotrphy is a progressive degenerative disease as a result of the loss of brain cells in the cerebellum which causes ataxia.

IV. Primary Lens Luxation (PLL)
Inherited from the Sealyham Terrier, though as of December 2018, the breed Statistics in the OFA.org database currently do not list any affected or carriers of the disease.

V. Cardiac
Often manifesting as Arrhythmias, but other conditions have been reported.

VI. Luxating Patella
Common in most small breed dogs, dogs affected with this will have a knee cap that will slip in and out of joint.

VII. Cancers
(ie. Lymphoma, Bladder Cancer)

VIII. vonWillebrand Type III
Inherited through the Scottish Terrier this is a specific mutation for the Scottish Terrier breed. It is a blood disorder.

IX. Epilepsy

X. Legg-Perthes Disease
Orthopedic condition of the head of femur bone where the blood vessels spontaneously fail to feed the bone causing degeneration.

XI. Degenerative Myelopathy
Another late onset disorder, it is a progressive & incurable disorder of the spinal cord.

XII. Congenital Deafness

XIII. Dry Eye Syndrome

XIV. Reproductive Issues.
Infertility of both male and female, Reabsorption, Pyometra

Cesky Terrier

3 GROOMING

Grooming the Cesky Terrier does require time and commitment to grooming. Because the coat keeps growing and genuinely is very low shedding, like most low shedding breeds, the unclipped coat will mat and the dog will be uncomfortable and the unbathed coat will develop an odor from the oil in its coat. Unlike other breeds however keeping a Cesky in show coat does not require more effort than keeping one as a well maintained pet. In fact, if you wish to keep your Cesky Terrier looking like the show dogs you see in pictures yourself, it just takes a little instruction, dedication, and practice. Be sure to consider the grooming commitment before adding a Cesky to your family, as professional grooming is a regular expense and even at-home grooming requires time and an investment in supplies and equipment.

Things to keep in mind:

*** The coat of the Cesky Terrier is silky and should have a metallic sheen.**

*** The furnishings should not be profuse.**

*** The hair on the body is left slightly longer than that on the head, shoulders and hind-quarters.**

*** Dental Care is important.**

If you choose to use a professional groomer, keep in mind that the many groomers are not familiar with this rare breed, so you may want to bring some pictures they can use as a guideline or recommend your groomer purchase a copy of this handbook, better yet, it makes a great gift!

Later in this chapter you will find detailed grooming instructions, including diagrams and suggested equipment for grooming yourself. In the long run, it is less expensive to groom yourself, but it does require an upfront investment in equipment (see list), and it takes some time and effort. If it is something you enjoy, it can be very rewarding and a lot of fun. If not, it is probably best left to a professional.

Brushing

The adult Cesky Terrier should be brushed and combed out at least three times a week. Combing is important, as brushing with a slicker brush alone does not remove tangles close to the skin. Before trimming, brush and comb your dog so all knots are gone. Inspect the pads of the foot and trim the hair between the pads as needed.

Regular brushing and combing is even more important for puppies, as puppy coats have a different texture and tend to mat more than adult coats. It is recommended that you brush/comb puppies daily, and be sure to brush/comb the hair in both directions to remove the smaller mats. Keeping up with the coat will make grooming a much more pleasant experience for you and the puppy. Combing a puppy daily takes about 5 minutes and is good training for adult grooming! You will find that once the adult coat comes in, matting is much less frequent or nonexistent if you are diligent about bathing and brushing. A regularly conditioned coat will remain hydrated and less likely to tangle.

If mats do develop, you can remove them carefully using the edge of the comb. It is recommended that you wash and use a deep conditioner first. You may use some spray, leave-in conditioner or detangle spray on the mats as well if they are severe, to help comb them out. Watch the armpits for mats as the rubbing when the dog moves may cause mats to develop. Wet weather can also cause matting. Mats are the number one reason some pet owners choose to keep the furnishings fairly short, especially in winter.

Bathing

Bathing can be done prior to clipping the dog, but can soothe the skin if done after clipping. If the dog gets particularly dirty in between, you may need to bathe before. In cold climates, blow dry after bathing. In warm climates, you may wish to let the dog air dry as this helps the coat and skin maintain hydration.

Use a good shampoo and follow with a conditioner to keep the coat healthy and make it easier to comb out. Be sure to rinse the dog well with warm water after shampooing and conditioning. Remember the Cesky Terrier has hair and not fur so it is often found that a human shampoo and conditioner has the proper pH balance.

Clipping

The Cesky is trimmed with electric clippers, **even for the show ring.** They are not hand-stripped like many terrier breeds. The traditional clipping pattern was designed to show off the combination of elegance and muscle tone that epitomizes the Cesky Terrier, and it was designed so it would not be difficult to maintain. Clipping frequency will depend on the speed at which your dog's coat grows. The average is approximately every two to four weeks.

<u>**Supplies**</u>

If you plan to use a professional groomer, you will still need some grooming essentials including:
Dog nail clippers or nail grinder (trim nails at least every one to two weeks)
Wire slicker brush (not too big, but long pins and relatively soft)
Metal comb (medium/fine or medium coarse)
Dog toothpaste and toothbrush or other dental care supplies
Styptic powder to stop bleeding in case you cut a nail too close
Small blunt tip hair scissor to trim between pads and tidy up between grooming sessions
Shampoo and Conditioner

*If you plan to groom yourself, you will need All of the above, **Plus** some additional supplies:*

Electric clippers with interchangeable blade heads
Oil or Cool Lube for clippers
Sanitizing spray for Clipper Blades
Blade #5F or #5FC
Blade #7F or #7FC
Blade #10
Blade #15
Blade #30
40+ tooth thinning shear or 40 tooth Blending shear (Double sided)
Medium Tooth Comb
Straight Shear blunt tip
Curved blunt tip shear
Brush (Medium Pin type)
A grooming table or other secure and accessible place to groom

The Cesky Terrier Grooming Step by Step for Companion or the Show Ring

The First Step should always be to brush your dog. If there are some stubborn knots or tangles do not force these out with a comb, slicker or brush.

2. Shampoo your Dog & use a Deep Conditioner

3. After a Bath and Deep Conditioning, brush your dog again to work out any last stubborn tangles.

4.It is recommended that you towel dry them as much as possible and then allow them to air dry, or blow dry on a low heat setting to prevent taking moisture out of the coat.

Prepare your grooming area.

The Cesky Terrier Grooming Pattern

The RED Section is clippered with a 7F blade starting at the occipital ridge and ending in a point 1 inch into the tail.

The **PURPLE** Section is clippered with a #10 blade starting at the brow line and meeting the 7F section at the occipital ridge.

The **GREEN** section is clippered with a #15 blade to highlight the musculature of the Cesky Terrier.

The EARS are typically trimmed with a #30 blade, but can also be trimmed with a #15 blade. This is determined by the fineness of the hair. Extremely Fine hair should not be trimmed with a #30 blade.

The **Dark BLUE** area is blended between the clippered area and the furnishings (skirt area). The hair of the skirt should not protrude past the thorax.

All section meeting lines should be blended so there is no visible transition to the naked eye. The legs are thinned to form a column. The feet are trimmed to be neat and hair removed between the paw pads.

Grooming the Head of the Cesky Terrier

The head of the Cesky Terrier is groomed to form a Blunt Wedge Shape. The hair is allowed to grow long from the brow forward towards the nose and slightly past.
This forms what is called a "Fall" and serves as protection for a hunting dog.
The Fall is trimmed slightly from the corner of the eye on the upper brow line to the middle of the eye on a diagonal, to be neatly blended into the Fall.
The Hair from the Middle of the lower eye line is brushed forward and trimmed at the nose line to create the blunt wedge shape.
The Hair from the middle of the eye to the outer corner of the eye is then Blended into the face in a neat transition. (purple section)

Additional Notes:

Cesky Terrier

4 BREED STANDARD

Below you will find the Standard of the Cesky terrier under FCI rules and guidelines. This standard is the ONLY standard recognized by the Cesky Terrier Club of America. The recommendation of the club is that Breeders and Judges alike adhere to this standard for the strict preservation of the Cesky Terrier breed, under the vision of the creator Frantisek Horak.

Important points highlighted in Red.

FCI-Standard N° 246

CZECH TERRIER
(Cesky Terrier)

TRANSLATION : Mrs Dipl. Ing. K. Bechov and Mrs R. BinderGresly.

ORIGIN : Czech Republic.

DATE OF PUBLICATION OF THE OFFICIAL VALID STANDARD : 11.03.1997.

UTILIZATION : Formerly a Terrier breed for hunting foxes and badgers, today more a house-and companion dog.

CLASSIFICATION FCI : Group   3 Terriers.

Section 2 Small sized Terriers.

Without working trial.

BRIEF HISTORICAL SUMMARY : The Czech Terrier is the result of an appropriate crossbreeding between a Sealyham Terrier dog and a Scotch Terrier bitch, with the aim to develop a light, short legged, well pigmented hunting Terrier, with practical drop ears, easy to groom and easy to train. In 1949 Mr. Frantisek Hor k from Kl novice near Prague started to improve the breed by fixing their characteristics. In 1959 these dogs were shown for the first time, and the breed was finally recognized by the FCI in 1963.

GENERAL APPEARANCE : Short legged, long haired, well made and well muscled Terrier with smallish drop ears, of a rectangular format.

IDEAL MEASURES :	Male	Female
Height at withers	29 cm	27 cm
Length of skull	21 cm	20 cm
Width of skull	10 cm	9 cm
Girth of thorax (behind elbows)	45 cm	44 cm
Length of body	43 cm	40cm

BEHAVIOUR / TEMPERAMENT : Balanced, non-aggressive, pleasant and cheerful companion, easy to train; somewhat reserved   towards strangers; of calm and kind disposition.

<u>HEAD</u>
Shaped like a long, blunt, not too broad wedge, the plane of the forehead forming a distinctive breaking with the bridge of the nose.

<u>CRANIAL REGION</u> :
<u>Skull</u> : Not too broad between the ears and tapering moderately towards the supraorbital ridges.   Occipital protuberance easy to palpate; cheek bones moderately prominent.   Frontal furrow only slightly marked.

<u>Stop</u> : Not accentuated but apparent.

<u>FACIAL REGION</u> :
<u>Nose</u> : Dark and well developed. It should be black on Terriers with a grey-blue coat and liver-coloured on light-coffee brown Terriers.

<u>Nasal bridge</u> : Straight.

<u>Jaws/teeth</u> : Strong jaws.   Scissors or level bite; complete dentition (the absence of the 2 M3 in the lower jaw not being penalized).

Teeth strong, regularly aligned and set square to
the jaw.

<u>Lips</u> : Relatively thick, fitting neatly.

<u>Cheeks</u> : Cheek bones not too prominent.

<u>Eyes</u> : Of medium size, slightly deep set, with a friendly expression; well covered by the overhanging eyebrows.   Brown or dark brown in grey-blue coated dogs, light   brown in light-coffee-brown dogs.

Eyelids black in grey-blue dogs, liver-colour in light-coffee-brown dogs.

<u>Ears</u> : Of medium size, dropping in such a way as to well cover the

orifice. Set on rather high and falling flat along the cheeks.

Shaped like a triangle, with the shorter side of the triangle at the fold of the ear.

<u>NECK</u> : Medium long, quite strong, carried on a slant. The skin at the throat is somewhat loose but without forming a dewlap.

<u>BODY</u> : Oblong.

<u>Upper line</u> : Not straight because loins and rump are always moderately arched.
<u>Withers</u> : Not very pronounced; neck set on rather high.

Back : Strong, of medium length.

<u>Loins</u> : Relatively long, muscular, broad and slightly rounded.

<u>Croup</u> : Strongly developed, muscular; pelvis moderately slanting.

Hip bones often slightly higher than the withers.

<u>Chest</u> : More cylindrical than deep; ribs well sprung.

<u>Belly</u> : Ample and slightly tucked up. Flanks well filled.

<u>TAIL</u> : The ideal length is 18-20 cm; relatively strong and low set. At rest hanging downward or with a slight bend at the tip; when alert the tail is carried sabre shape horizontally or higher.

<u>LIMBS</u>

<u>FOREQUARTERS</u> : The forelegs should be straight, well boned and parallel.

<u>Shoulders</u> : Muscular.

<u>Elbows</u> : Somewhat loose, yet neither turned in nor out.

<u>Forefeet</u> : Large; well arched toes and strong nails. Pads well developed and thick.

<u>HINDQUARTERS</u> : Hindlegs strong, parallel, well angulated and muscular.

<u>Lower thigh</u> : Short.
<u>Hock joint</u> : Set relatively high, strongly developed.

<u>Hindfeet</u> : Smaller than the forefeet.

<u>GAIT / MOVEMENT</u> : Free, enduring, vigorous, with drive. Gallop rather slow but lasting. The forelegs extend in a straight forward line.

<u>SKIN</u> : Firm, thick, without wrinkles or dewlap, pigmented.

<u>COAT</u>

<u>TEXTURE</u> : Hair long, fine but firm, slightly wavy with a silky gloss; not too much overdone. The Czech Terrier is groomed by scissors (clipping). At the forepart of the head the hair is not to be clipped thus forming brows and beard. On the lower parts of the legs, under the chest and belly the hair should not be clipped either. In show condition the hair at the upper side of the neck, on the shoulders and on the back should not be longer than 1 - 1,5 cm; it should be shorter on the sides of the body and on the tail and quite short on the ears, cheeks, at the lower side of the neck, on elbows, thighs and round the vent. The transition between clipped and unclipped areas should be pleasing for the eye and never abrupt.

COLOUR : The Czech Terrier has 2 varieties of coat colour :

- grey-blue (puppies are born black)
- light-coffee-brown (puppies born chocolate brown)

In both colour varieties yellow, grey or white markings are permitted on the head (beard, cheeks), neck, chest, belly, the limbs and round the vent. Sometimes there is also a white collar or a white tip of the tail. The basic colour, however, must always be predominant.

HEIGHT AND WEIGHT :

Height at withers between 25 - 32 cm. Ideal size for a dog = 29 cm, for a bitch = 27 cm.

The weight must not be less than 6 kg and more than 10 kg.

FAULTS : Any departure from the foregoing points should be considered a fault and the seriousness with which the fault should be regarded should be in exact proportion to its degree and its effect upon the health and welfare of the dog.

- Weak construction.
- Temporary loss of nasal pigmentation (snow nose).
- Weak, short or snipey foreface, with weakly developed teeth.
- Absence of one (1) incisor.
- Eyes too big or protruding.
- Ears too big or too small, or different in shape or carriage as described in the standard.
- Back too long or too short.
- Crooked forelegs, incorrect front.
- Coat too fine or too coarse.

DISQUALIFYING FAULTS :

- Aggresive or overly shy.
- Any dog clearly showing physical or behavioural abnormalities shall be disqualified.

- Absence of more than 4 teeth altogether; absence of 2 or more incisors.
- Canine placed in vestibulo position.
- Entropion or ectropion.
- Chest circumference more than 50 cm.
- Curled tail or carried over the back.
- Long brindled coat on dogs older than 2 years.
- Coarse or curled cotton-wool type hair.
- White markings covering more than 20%; white blaze on the head.
- Irregular, jerky, spasmodic movements ("Scottie cramp")
- Weight above 10 kg or less than 6 kg.
- Shyness, unbalanced or aggressive disposition.

N.B:

- Male animals should have two apparently normal testicles fully descended into the scrotum.
- Only functionally and clinically healthy dogs, with breed typical conformation, should be used for breeding.

St-FCI n°246/20.01.1998

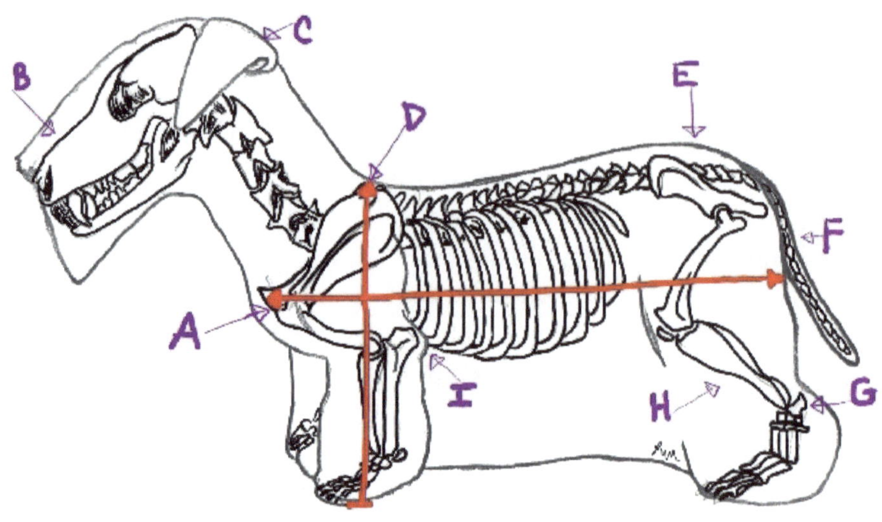

A. Point of Shoulder
B. Nasal Bridge
C. Ear
D. Withers/Top of Shoulder
E. Croup (Rump)
F. Tail
G. Hock Joint
H. Lower thigh
 I. Elbow

5 JUDGING THE CESKY TERRIER

The most important thing to consider when judging the Cesky Terrier is Size. The Cesky is a Short Legged terrier. This terrier should be small enough to fit into burrows that a Sealyham would not be capable of fitting into, and yet have enough leg to cover ground. The measurement of the front leg bones, from elbow to point of shoulder and the bones from elbow to ankle, should be should be equal. The ideal Height at the withers : male = 29 cm (11.4 inches) and female = 27cm (10.6 inches). Height should not exceed 32 cm (12.5 inches). This is to be a muscular but lean terrier, and it should be agile not bulky or cumbersome. The weight can not be less than 6 kg (13.23 pounds) or higher than 10 kg (22 pounds).

The second thing to consider is ratio of height and length. The Cesky is of a long low, rectangular format. The height (point of withers to the ground) to length (from point of shoulder to point of buttock) ratio should equal 1 : 1.5. The Cesky is not to be of a square nor a tall rectangular format.

For example a male of the ideal height 29 cm (11.4 inches), the body length should equal 43.5 cm (17.1 inches). In judging the Cesky terrier it is important to remember the overall ratio is important. In the next chapter we will discuss type, in the Cesky terrier breed there are two basic types. ***It is important at this point to note that being able to recognize these measurements is important as the two types become visually deceiving because of length of rib cage.*** The standard allows for both a shorter and longer rib cage, which visually will give a more compact or a lengthier appearance. The reason for this is the difference in type.   However when compared up against one another, the two types, though visually different should measure the same. A second area to note is that color (darker gray versus light) will also visually change perception.

Topline is the next in consideration of the breed, and the correct topline is essential for the work ability of this breed. A roaching topline should always be dismissed for lack of merit. Cesky terriers who have a roaching topline will not have **the proper tilt of pelvis**. The topline is also NOT achieved by poor angulation of the rear. The topline is achieved by the angle of the pelvis and the longer length of the bone from stifle to pelvis joint. In a proper Cesky this bone in the rear legs will be longer than the bone from stifle to hock joint. The rear should be moderately angulated.

If the Cesky has proper movement the rising topline will be maintained when moving. To obtain the smooth graceful movement the elbows will **not** be set close to the body. They should be set just past the thorax, in order to allow freedom of movement alongside the body. The elbows however should not protrude from the body (not be turned out).

The dentition of the Cesky should be full, with the lower M3 teeth permitted to be missing. The bite should be scissor or level. Malocclusion of the Canine teeth, is a disqualifying fault.

The color of the Cesky, is the hallmark of the breed and **is to be predominantly Gray in color**. The Cesky over the age of 2 years old will not have brindle in the long coat. Stripes in the short cut areas of the coat may be present until the age of 3 years old.   After this time the coat should be clear of stripes.

The Cesky can have silver or tan markings in the areas of the lower leg, the vent, chest and lower jaw only. The Cesky can have white markings, equaling no more than 20 percent of the body color, and located only on the legs, chest, vent, neck and lower jaw. There should never be a white blaze on the head or back of the neck. The reason for the specific expression of these markings is due to the inheritance of the expression from the Black and Tan Scottish terrier that was seen in the 1940s and 50s. For photographs of Black and Tan Scottish terriers, please see the Cesky Club of America's Mentor Group on Facebook or contact the club directly.

Separately, the saddle tan pattern (RALY gene) as seen in the welsh terrier, was introduced into the breed by an impure breeding in 1972 (per writings of the creator and the knowledge of color genetics of the parent breeds Sealyham and Scottish terrier, neither of which carry the RALY gene).

While it has become acceptable to allow a saddle pattern in light and dark gray, which is in keeping with the standard description of predominantly gray, Saddle tan and black or saddle tan and dark gray are not acceptable by the standard. The predominately gray Cesky Terrier, should be unique unto itself and should never be confused with another breed such as the Lucas Terrier, which was also created in the 1940s using a Norfolk and Sealyham terrier.

The Cesky Terrier should not fade to white, nor should it remain black. A puppy born white or marked with more than 20 percent white, or has faded to white, should never be bred or exhibited and should be Disqualified per the standard.

A Cesky should never resemble a gray version of its parent breeds. The Cesky traits are unique to itself and as such the grooming should also be notably so.

The Texture of the Cesky coat should be fine, silky and can have a slight wave. The Adult Cesky coat, should never be cotton like or have a wool like texture, and should not be thick strands, overly profuse, or coarse. A puppy may have a cotton like texture that may change with age. The hair would be considered profuse if it exceeds the basic body lines, from the side view, the rear view and from the view above. There should be not be a noticeable transition or marked lines of the areas of varying length.

The Cesky should have triangular shape ears that are not heavy or overly large. They should also not be so small, break or be set so high that they resemble those of a wire fox or welsh terrier. The ear however, should break slightly above the skull.

The neck of a Cesky should be long and carried in a graceful arch, not an upright position. The head should appear to be a blunt wedge, or axe shape. The Rib cage is cylindrical and well sprung. The tail should be set low, with low carriage preferred. The tail should be seen as an extension of the body line's wave. The tail can be carried higher in position but not given higher importance nor be a measurement of temperament in this breed. The tail carried very high in a position over the back (squirreling) is a disqualifying fault. A tucked tail however should never be rewarded as the breed should be cautious but never timid.

A "Black and Tan" Cesky Terrier is visually grey with silver or light tan markings in the pattern described as in the standard, on the lower leg, lower jaw, chest and vent.

6 BREEDING & GENETICS:
MANAGING MUTATIONS & TYPE

The Cesky Terrier is an Inbred Breed.

According to the records of Mr. Horak, just two and half dogs contributed genetic material to the Foundation of the Breed (Also known as Line 1A). (The second Sealyham was son of the first, so only half of his genes were unique (those contributed to him by his mother). A second branch of this Foundation. (Line 1B) we will discuss later.

Unlike other breeds you can not look to other kennels or countries to expand the gene pool. Today the most respected breeders fully understand that very selective breeding to maintain consistency, as well as the attributes of the breed standard, is a matter of selection for expression of the limited genes contributed by the foundation dogs and tracking genetic mutations that occur in each generation.

We should note that a mutation of a gene does not change the protein that creates the gene, merely effects the expression and or function of that gene. The only way to introduce new genetic material (new genes) to the gene pool is to introduce a completely unrelated dog. As such the Cesky is accepted to have a very high COI, and factoring COI is not a main factor.

In the most simplest explanation, without giving a full course on genetics, we have developed a Foundation Chart so that one can understand the limited gene pool within the cesky breed.

It is well recognized, that each offspring will inherit half its genetic material from its mother and half from their father.

The Cesky Terrier (Line 1A) began with the Cross of a Sealyham and a Scottish Terrier.

Buganier Urquelle (Sealyham) x Scotch Rose (Scottish Terrier)

From this mating Balda Lovu zdar was born.

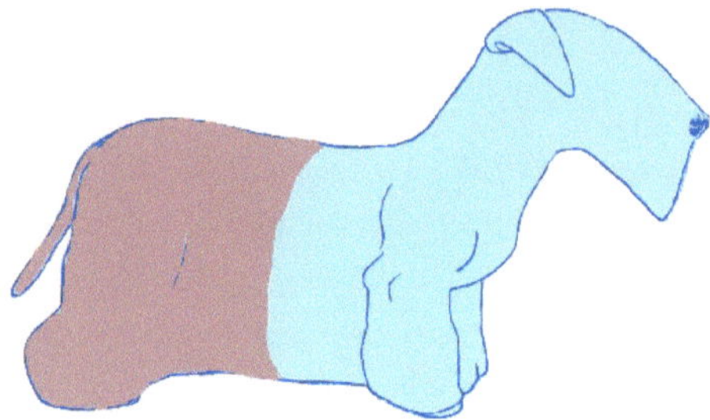

Balda was brindle, like his mother Scotch Rose. Purposely, he was bred to his mother Scotch Rose.

This mating, resulted in Diana Lovu zdar. This female had the desired traits and resemblance of the Cesky Terrier type.

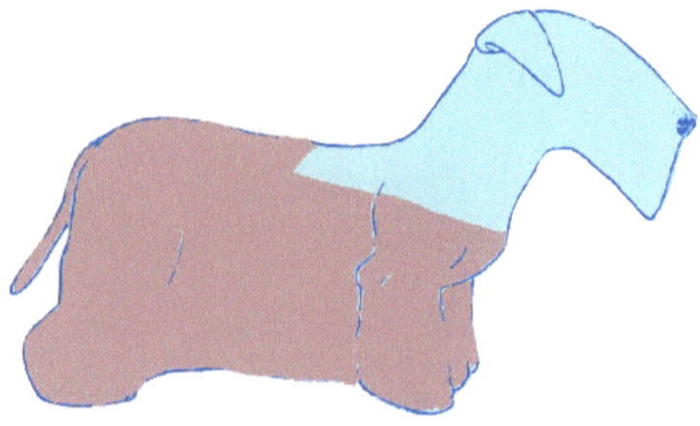

Diana, going forward was bred to Jasans Amorous Artilleryman, a Sealyham terrier who was son of Buganier Urguelle, (he is represented by half Blue, the genes of his father, and purple from his mother who would be the last to contribute new genetic material to the 1A line).

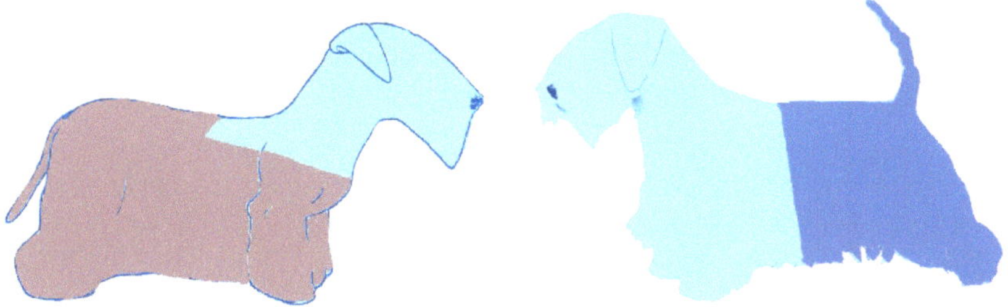

The mating produced Fantom and Fenka Lovu zDar.

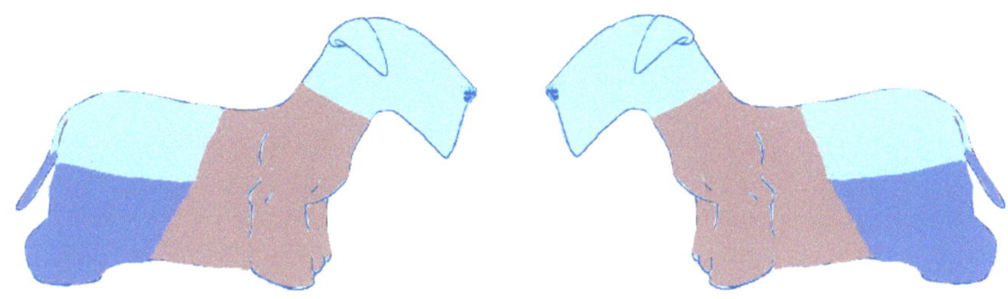

Fantom and Fenka carried gene contributions from each of the genetic donors.

In 1956, Fenka and Fantom were bred to together and produced one single female Halali Lovu zDar.

In 1958, two breedings would occur.
Halali was bred to her father Fantom, and Diana was bred to her son Fantom. Both breedings resulted in Brown Cesky terriers. The breeding of Halali to Fantom produced Chytry Lovu zdar a brown and tan dog. He was not recorded as being used for breeding. However his littermate Chrabra was. None of the puppies produced by Fantom and Diana would be bred.
The gene which produces Brown and brown and tan was previously assumed to be inherited from the Sealyham, it is now explained with genetic data, to be inherited from the Scottish terrier.

In 1959, the breeding of Halali and Fantom was repeated, producing 4 puppies, but it would be only Javor who would be kept in the breeding program.

In 1960 & 1961 Javor would be bred to his sister from the 1958 litter, Chrabra.
It would be from the 1961 litter, that two females would be kept for the breeding program. Lovka and Lapka.

In 1962, Javor was bred to his mother Halai and four puppies were born. From this litter it would be Mrak that would be the one to contribute to the breed development.
In fact it would be Lovka, Lapka and Ulrika and Urana, (daughters of Mrak and Chrabra, 1966) which would form the four basic families from which all other Cesky Terriers would descend.

Lovka was designated above all by Mr. Horak, as correct breed type. Lovka was stout, with a wonderful coat, and lower set tail which she carried in the preferred lower saber position. Lapka her littermate was small and energetic with a high carried tail. In spite of these qualities it would be Lapka that would produce offspring of the preferred type.

Here we will note that, an impure breeding occurred in 1972, resulting in the litter that produced Dolly Vivat. The breeding introduced traits not desired in the cesky terrier breed. (longer leg length, undesirable texture, and the infamous RALY gene which controls the expression of saddle tan). The cesky that are descendants of cesky from this litter formed the 1B line.

In 1984 & 1985, one more Sealyham, a female named Andra z Rastamoru would be bred to the Cesky terrier Vanek Lovu zDar to contribute genetic material to try and bring back the preferred breed traits back to the 1B line of Cesky terriers. With just 3 or 5 dogs (depending on whether you breed from both Line1A and 1B lines or just Line 1A) available as the entire gene pool with which to work, today the most respected breeders understand that very selective breeding to maintain consistency, as well as the attributes of the breed standard is a matter of selection for expression of genes and tracking genetic mutations.

Within the cesky breed there are two basic types, one is moderate boned, and has a bit longer rib cage, which   creates the appearance of a moderate loin. The neck is well arched and often has a more elegant head. Often described as the "Scottie" type, the overall visual appearance projects as a more compact terrier. The other type, often described as the "Sealyham" type, has a slightly shorter rib cage, which gives the appearance of a longer loin. The bone on this type generally is a bit heavier, and the head more coarse. Both types are acceptable within the measurements of the standard and are needed within the breed and should be carefully cross bred to maintain the standard.

Genetically the breed color is effected by many genes, Including the following known mapped Genes:

E Locus (ie. E/E, E^M/E^M)
The E^M/E^M, gene is the gene for masking. In the Cesky Terrier this can be a dark mask of charcoal grey or a silver mask that may or may not blend into the rest of the coat.

K Locus (ie K^B/K^B, K^B/k^y , k^y/k^{br})
The Scottish Terrier, Scotch Rose was a carrier of the brindle gene, k^{br}, If a cesky puppy expresses Brindle during color change (affected by the I & G Locus), the puppy will always be brindle genetically. However, by standard only those Cesky terriers that visually clear by the age of 2 years are acceptable. This visually happens when the coat is affected enough by Intensity and Graying (I & G Loci) that the stripes merely blend into the color of the main coat.

A Locus (Effects Patterning) (a^t/a^t, a/a, a/a^t)
a^t/a^t is The gene responsible for Two Tone & Black and Tan. The Cesky Terrier inherited the a^t recessively from both the Scottish terrier, and the Sealyham Terrier. From the Scottish Terrier it expresses as Black and Tan (see page 33) because of the inheritance, and from the Sealyham Terrier this gene in combination with another expresses as two tone as seen in Picture on Page 40, this was inherited by the Sealyham from its ancestor the Dandie Dinmont. The second gene that causes the

expression of pattern with the a^t/a^t gene has not yet been identified. When a Cesky Terrier Inherits the K^B/K^B gene, the a^t/a^t Black and Tan expression (from the Scottie) will be suppressed.

B Locus (Controls Black and Brown, BB (black) bb (brown) Bb (Black, carrying brown)

I Locus (Intensity Gene) &
G Locus (Greying Gene)
The combination of the I and G Loci are what cause the Cesky Terrier to turn Grey. If either or both Genes are dormant the Cesky puppy will not change from Black to Grey, it will remain black. Similarly if either or both genes are of strong expression the Cesky puppy will turn white with age.
Neither of these genes can be currently tested for, and breeders must be careful to note the inheritance from the parents as well as the grandparents of the puppy.
S Locus (White spotting or Full White Color)

Additional the 1B line has introduced, by the impure breeding, the active or carried (RALY) gene (The RALY gene is the gene responsible for the expression of Saddle Tan). The pure 1A line will always have the N/N result when testing for this gene.
Cesky Terrier from the 1B line who are K^B/k^y and have inherited the a^t/a^t and active (RALY) gene will express as Saddle Tan and Black/Gray, this expression is not accepted by the standard.

7 CESKY TERRIER IN THE USA

Important Firsts:
- The breed was first imported into the USA in the 1980s by a group of enthusiasts, including Sue Young, Connie Beach and Lori Moody.
- The first club was formed by these enthusiasts: The Cesky Terrier Club of America (CTCA), in January 1988.
- Connie Beach served as the First President of CTCA.
- The Cesky Terrier was able to compete in the American Kennel Club terrier group starting 30th June, 2011.
- The only Certificate of Merit earned by a Cesky Terrier: Devineheart's Babicka at Altrincham – "Katrina", Owned by Loren & Gloria Marino, under Judge William F. Potter, II
- The first Championship points awarded to a Cesky Terrier occurred on 1st of July 2011, by Judge Desmond Murphy.
- The First Championship was obtained on August 6, 2011 at a show in North Carolina, by Devineheart's Babicka at Altrincham – "Katrina", under Judge Kenneth McDermott.
- The First Grand Championship was obtained on October 8, 2011 , in Exton , PA, by Devineheart's Babicka at Altrincham – "Katrina", under Judge Seymour Weiss.
- Only two Cesky Terriers from the USA were invited to the First Westminster Kennel club the Cesky was eligible to compete:
    1. Devineheart's Babicka at Altrincham – "Katrina",
    2. Tryska Von Klanovice – "Nadia"
- First Bronze Grand Champion June 24, 2012: Devineheart's Babicka at Altrincham – "Katrina", under Judge Dr. Hugh Scott Kellogg
- First Bred By Exhibitor Champion: October 19, 2014,

Altrincham Act Four Scene Two – "Viktor" under Judge Kristen Francis
- First Best in Show (Brace) October 5, 2012: Devineheart's Babicka at Altrincham – "Katrina" & Tryska von Klanovice -- "Nadia", BOB under Judge: Rosalind Kramer, BIS under Judge Kathleen Steen
- First Cesky Best of Breed at the Historic Morris & Essex Kennel Club: October 8, 2015, Milenka's Hector in Act Four – "Hector", under Judge Kathleen Ferris.
- #1 Ranked Cesky Terrier in the Breed in 2011 & 2012 : Devineheart's Babicka at Altrincham – "Katrina"

Since the Breed's Recognition there has been great opposition to its growth by a small group of people. As such the breed has failed to thrive, efforts have been thwarted to recruit new exhibitors and experienced breeders and many people have walked away from the breed.

The Cesky Terrier Club of America however has maintained its purpose in educating new owners, trying to recruit experienced breeders to aid in the preservation of the breed and to educate judges around the world. The Cesky Terrier Club of America will and has always strived to maintain the standard, preserve the vision of Mr. Horak, and to breed a healthy companion.

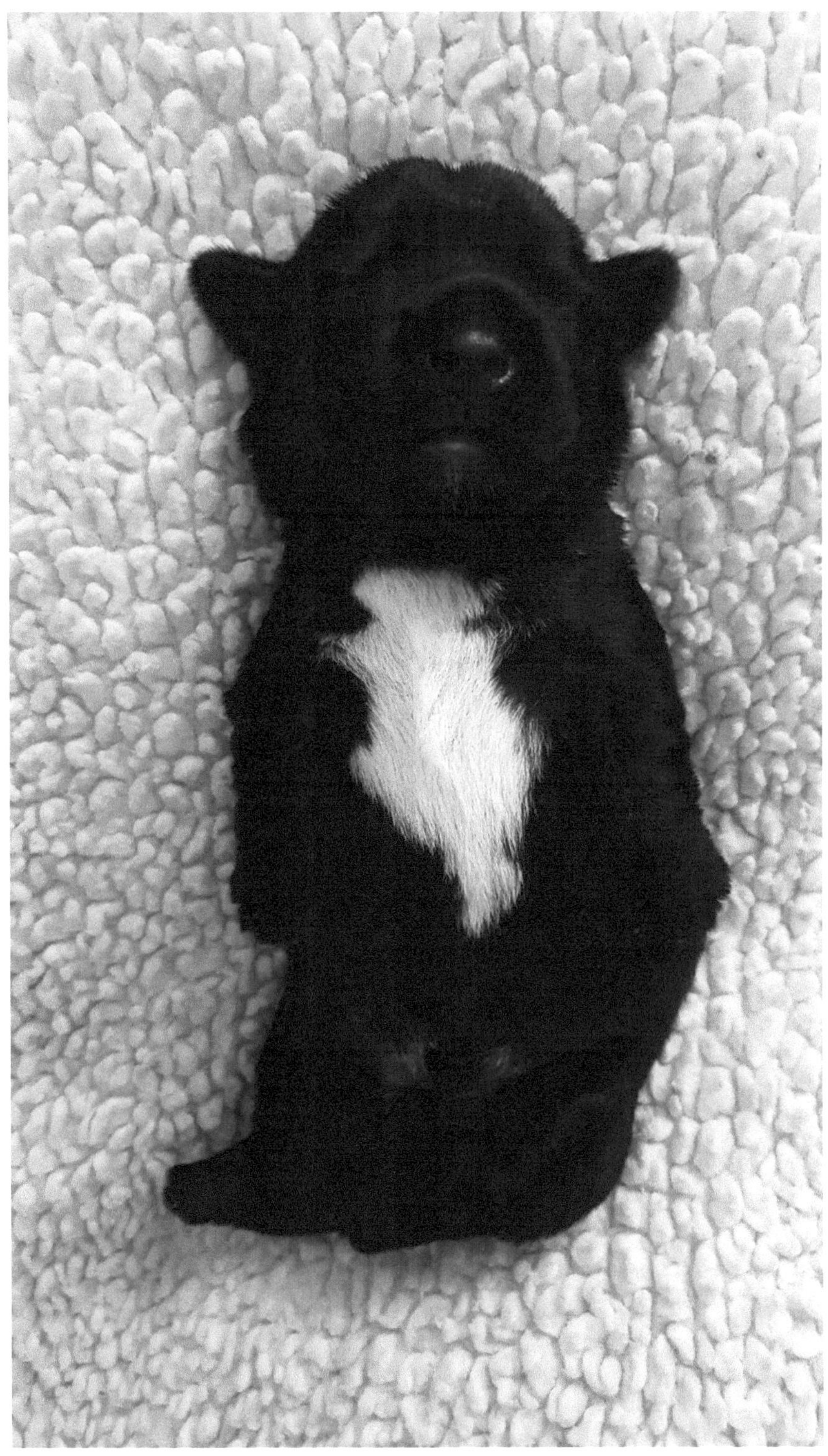

Cesky Terrier

The Cesky Terrier Club of America would like to
Thank you for taking time to
Learn About this Unique Breed!

Cesky Terrier

56